Contents

Introduction

Festivals are celebrations when families and friends look forward to the future and remember events that have happened in the past.

This street **parade** is to celebrate the Jewish festival of Purim.

Many festivals are held in holy places such as **churches** and **temples**, and others are held in the streets of villages and cities, where people gather to have fun.

This family is celebrating the Jewish festival of Hannukkah in their home.

Some festivals are celebrated at home, when families get together to share special days.

Festivals of Light

Light plays an important part in many festivals all over the world.

During Diwali, Hindus light candles and small lights called **divas**.

Diwali
Diwali means a row or garland of lights. It marks the start of the Hindu New Year and lasts for five days.

A candle is lit for each night of Hannukkah on a special candlestick called a menorah.

FESTIVAL DIARY

Hannukkah
Jewish
December

Diwali
Hindu
Late October or early November

Hannukkah

Hannukkah is the Jewish festival of light. This festival lasts for eight days.

Lamps and Lights

Lanterns as well as candles are often used to celebrate festivals.

In the evening of Teng Chieh, people hang lanterns from tall poles and carry them in a procession.

Teng Chieh

Teng Chieh comes at the end of the Chinese New Year's celebrations. It is a time when families look forward to spring.

During the Buddhist Festival of Lights, families visit **shrines** and say prayers.

Buddhist Festival of Lights
This festival ends with a procession of 1001 lights. People chant and ring bells and give out strips of red cloth for good luck.

FESTIVAL DIARY

Teng Chieh
China
February

Festival of Lights
Buddhist
February

Remembering

Some festivals are held to remember and celebrate stories from the past.

Matza is a type of flat bread that Jewish people eat at Pesach.

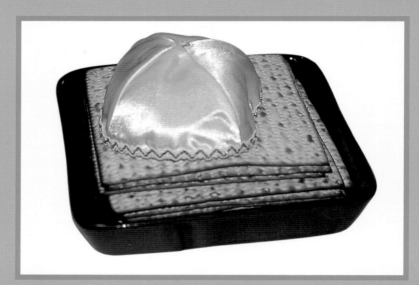

Pesach

Pesach remembers the time when the Jews escaped from **slavery** in Egypt. It is also known as Passover.

Children wear costumes to act out the parts of the Purim story in the **synagogue**.

Purim

Purim is a festival where Jews remember a time long ago when they were saved from a wicked man, called Haman, by a queen, called Esther.

FESTIVAL DIARY

Pesach
Jewish
Between March and April

Purim
Jewish
End of February or early March

11

Holy Days

The year is full of holy days that are very important to different religions.

After Eid ul-Fitr, people go to the **mosque** to say special prayers.

Eid ul-Fitr

The festival of Eid ul-Fitr celebrates the end of the Muslim holy month of **Ramadan**.

Jewish families gather for a feast the day before Yom Kippur.

Yom Kippur

Yom Kippur is the holiest day of the Jewish year. This is the day when Jews ask for God's forgiveness for the bad things they may have done.

FESTIVAL DIARY

Eid ul-Fitr
Muslim
December

Yom Kippur
Jewish
October

Children's Days

Many festivals around the world are just for children.

Girls dress in their best clothes during Hina Matsuri.

Hina Matsuri

The Japanese Girls' Festival, called Hina Matsuri, is also known as the Dolls' Festival or the Peach Blossom Festival.

Children dress up in traditional Turkish clothes and perform special dances and songs for Egemenlik Bayrami.

Egemenlik Bayrami

Egemenlik Bayrami is also known as International Children's Day. Children fly kites, watch puppet shows and eat sweet, sticky cakes.

FESTIVAL DIARY

Hina Matsuri
Japan
5 May

Egemenlik Bayrami
Turkey
23 April

Growing Up

Almost every society celebrates the time when children reach a special age.

When a person has been confirmed, he or she can take part in **communion**.

Confirmation

In Christian religions, the service of confirmation marks the change from child to adult. It is usually held when a person reaches his or her early teens

During Amrit Sanskar, the person is sprinkled with a sacred drink, called amrit.

Amrit Sanskar

When a Sikh person is around 14 or 16 years old, they can become part of a special community called the Khalsa. This is celebrated in a ceremony called Amrit Sanskar.

FESTIVAL FACT

After Amrit Sanskar, family and friends eat a sacred Sikh pudding together from one bowl.

Child to Adult

The time when a child becomes an adult is very special for families around the world.

During Bar Mitzvah, a boy carries and reads from the Jewish **sacred** book, called the **Torah**.

Bar Mitzvah

Under Jewish law, a boy becomes an adult at the age of 13. The ceremony to celebrate this is called Bar Mitzvah.

A girl reads from the Torah in Hebrew, the Jewish language, at her Bat Mitzvah.

Bat Mitzvah

The ceremony where Jewish girls become adults is called Bat Mitzvah. It is held when a girl reaches the age of 12.

Getting Engaged

Engagements celebrate when a couple promises to marry one another.

The engagement ring is put on the fourth finger of the bride's left hand.

Christian engagement

In a Christian engagement, the man gives his future bride a special ring.

20

The bride is given a **sari** and a scarf, called a dupatta, by her mother-in-law.

Hindu engagement

In a Sikh or Hindu engagement the families of the bride and groom meet at a special ceremony, called Rokna.

FESTIVAL FACT

After Rokna, another Sikh ceremony is held for women only. It is called Chunni.

Getting Married

Weddings are special events when a man and woman become husband and wife.

The groom at a Sikh wedding carries a special sword.

Sikh wedding

At a Sikh wedding, the bride wears a red dress. Red is believed to be a lucky colour for women.

The bride has patterns drawn on her feet and her hands with a special dye, called **henna**.

Muslim wedding

During a Muslim wedding, the couple agrees to marry one another three times and then the bride and groom give each other a ring.

FESTIVAL FACT

The **Qu'ran**, the Muslim holy book, is read at a Muslim wedding and the **Imam** gives a talk about marriage.

Down the Aisle

Weddings are times of great joy for the families and friends of the bride and groom.

The bride and groom are blessed at the altar at the front of the church.

Christian wedding

Christian weddings usually take place in a church. After the ceremony, rice and confetti are thrown over the couple for good luck.

A Jewish couple stands beneath a canopy, called the hupah, during the wedding.

Jewish wedding

During a Jewish wedding in a synagogue the couple shares one glass of wine. The groom then breaks the glass by stamping on it.

FESTIVAL FACT

The hupah is made from a fine cloth that is draped over some poles and covered in flowers.

Mother's Day

This celebration is held around the world to say thank you to mothers for everything they do.

Families give presents and flowers to their mothers to celebrate Mother's Day.

Ancient Greece
Mother's Day dates from ancient Greece and has been celebrated for thousands of years.

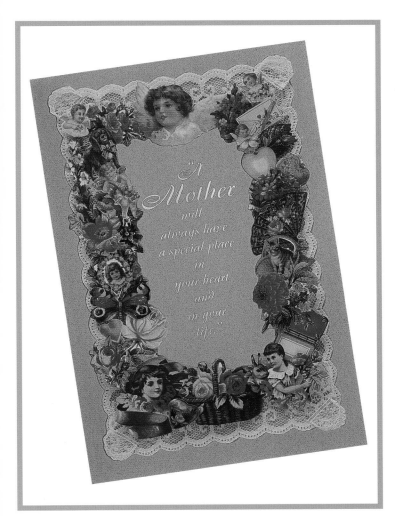

Mothers are also given a card on Mother's Day.

Around the world

Today, many countries hold Mother's Days at different times of the year.

FESTIVAL DIARY

Mother's Day
United Kingdom
March

Mother's Day
United States
Second Sunday in May

Fête de Màres
France
Last Sunday in May

Mata Tiritha Puja
Nepal
End of April or early May

Try This!

Ask an adult to help you with these activities.

Make a menorah for Hannukkah

You will need:

- coloured pencils or felt-tip pens
- paint brushes and paint
- white paper
- scissors
- PVA glue and glue brush
- sticky tape

1 Draw the outline of a menorah onto a large sheet of paper.

2 Colour it in with gold or yellow paint. Fix it to a wall with sticky tape.

3 Draw eight flames on a sheet of white paper.

4 Paint the flames yellow or gold with red centres.

5 Ask an adult to cut out the flames. Each day of Hannukkah, stick one of the flames onto one of the candles. After eight days your menorah will be completely lit.

Make a Mother's Day card

You will need:

- paint brushes and paint
- glitter
- pipe cleaners

- PVA glue
- glue brush
- two sheets of card

1 Paint some flowers onto a folded sheet of card, leaving enough space to spell out the word 'Mum' at the top.

2 Bend the pipe cleaners to form the letters of the word 'MUM'. Stick the pipe cleaners onto the other sheet of card and leave to dry.

3 Use the paint brush to cover the letters with paint.

4 Place the wet letters face down at the top of your card and press down firmly. Then pull the card away to see the word.

5 Decorate your card by putting very small dabs of glue on it and sprinkling glitter over it. Write your own message inside your card.

How to Say...

Bar Mitzvah
say *bar mits-va*

Bat Mitzvah
say *bat mits-va*

Chunni
say *chu-nee*

Diwali
say *di-wa-lee*

Egemenlik Bayrami
say *e-ge-men-lik bay-rar-mee*

Eid ul-Fitr
say *ay-eed ool-fitr*

Hannukkah
say *ha-na-ka*

Hina Matsuri
say *hee-na mat-soo-ree*

Hupah
say *hu-pa*

Mata Tiritha Puja
say *ma-ta ti-ree-ta poo-ja*

Pesach
say *pe-sak*

Qu'ran
say *kor-ran*

Teng Chieh
say *teng chee-eh*

Torah
say *tor-ra*

Yom Kippur
say *yom ki-pur*

Glossary

Church
A Christian place of worship.

Communion
A Christian religious ceremony when wine and wafers are eaten.

Divas
Small lanterns that are given out during Diwali, the Hindu festival of light.

Henna
A reddish-brown dye that is made from the leaves of the henna plant. The dye is used to make patterns on the hands and feet of a Muslim bride.

Imam
A Muslim religious leader.

Matza
A type of flat bread eaten at the Jewish festival of Pesach.

Mosque
A Muslim place of worship.

Parade
A march or procession of bands, floats, vehicles and people.

Qu'ran
The Muslim holy book.

Ramadan
The Muslim sacred month of prayer and fasting.

Sacred
Something is called sacred if it is thought to be holy.

Sari
A dress from Asia made from one long piece of cloth.

Shrine
A place that may contain sacred objects and is thought to be holy.

Slavery
When a person is owned by another and is forced to work for little or no pay.

Synagogue
A Jewish place of worship.

Temple
A building that is used for prayer.

Torah
The Jewish holy book.

Index